Leadership in the '80s

Leadership in the '80s:

ESSAYS ON HIGHER EDUCATION

by

Chris Argyris

and

Richard M. Cyert

with Comments by

Stephen K. Bailey and Gene I. Maeroff

IEM

INSTITUTE FOR EDUCATIONAL MANAGEMENT
Harvard University
Cambridge, Massachusetts

International Standard Book Number: 0 – 934222–01–0
Library of Congress Catalog Card Number: 80–80425

Published by:
Institute for Educational Management
Harvard University
Cambridge, Massachusetts 02138

TABLE OF CONTENTS

Preface

Stephen K. Bailey

Once upon a time there may have been a golden age for college and university presidents—an age when perquisites, trustee confidence, faculty deference, student respect, institutional autonomy, and general public support for higher education combined to fill academic leaders with an Olympian status and with a sense of manifest influence and destiny. Some would identify the first half of the twentieth century as such an age when, in the words of Harlan Cleveland, the "exhilaration exceeded the exhaustion." But no one would make such claims for the past fifteen years—or for the next ten. College and university presidents are presently and prospectively a beleaguered lot. Most of their institutions are faced with shrinking enrollments and shrinking resources in an inflation-ridden economy. Beset more and more by monitoring and regulatory impulses from near and distant governing and coordinating authorities, sapped by the contentiousness and litigiousness of faculty and students, battered by conflicting inside and outside pressures on such intractable issues as equity in athletics and divestment in South Africa, worn down by internal adversary proceedings that diminish a distantly remembered sense of collegiality, depressed by the bone weariness attendant on relentless conflict resolution, college and university presidents struggle to keep their noses above water, let alone their souls on top.

There are surely a few who find psychic satisfaction in nibbling down the inches of paper in their in-baskets, discovering ways to soften the impact of budgetary decrements, or humoring colleagues down from highs of anger. But for every resilient and ebullient administrator there must be a hundred filled with self-doubt and with a vague and corrosive bewilderment. The fact is that for many it is not very much fun anymore. They continue from a sense of duty, from a reluctance to lost status, from an often meritless hope that things will somehow become easier. But their eyes become less luminous, reminding all of us that few sadnesses of the world exceed the act of witnessing clear lenses of vision being scratched into opaqueness by the abrasions of contentious minutiae.

The next decade of administrators will be challenged time and again by Charles Eliot's reminder that the prime requisite of their success will be "their willingness to give pain."

This, then, is the rather lugubrious cyclorama against which the following essays are staged. The two formal essays are complementary. The lucid summary by Gene Maeroff suggests the richness of the discourse prompted by the essays themselves. There is an emerging central theme:

quick fixes will not work; salvation is achieved, partly by grace, but mostly by the hard work of pondering fundamental questions and positing anew the essential values of the academy. Such values transcend questions of curriculum and structure. They are as applicable to two-year public institutions as they are to major research universities. They are encapsulated in two phrases: "disciplined thought" and "the civilized treatment of others."

"Disciplined thought" is the hallmark of higher learning. It implies a respect for evidence, for the canons of logic, for sensitivity to the nuances of language, for loosely held and remediable hypotheses, for proven skills. It is the enemy of grade inflation, of verbal slobbery, of undiscriminating judgments. When colleges and universities forget their ultimate roots in disciplined thought, they become worse than meretricious. They set loose a powerful and sinister cynicism that erodes and corrodes the enveloping society. President Cyert is particularly worried that the competition for students in the proximate years ahead will induce the higher academy to substitute easy certification for proven merit. The long-range consequences: a world filled with academic "Kentucky Colonels."

Colleges and universities take pride in their role of preserving and enhancing "civilized values." But those of us who have spent our lives in academic settings know that the academy can be cruel, arbitrary, unfeeling, and manipulative. As budgets get tighter, as enrollments decline, as new claims for social justice [by minorities, women, the handicapped, and the elderly] press relentlessly on administrators, faculty, and staff, neurotic manifestations of fears can only exacerbate interpersonal cussedness. Unless a conscious search is made for what Professor Argyris calls double-loop learning, college and university executives will attempt to finesse the growing fears with the tricks and fixes of manipulative management. Predictably, this will only heighten the cynicism and deepen the trauma. In times of crisis, where a Hobbesian war of "all against all" is pending, great leadership by act and by example reaches for radical unities. In such circumstances, the civilized treatment of others does not imply trying to please everyone. It means building trust by sharing dilemmas and by allowing "multiple" but not "infinite" inputs to decisions. Above all it means searching for what Edmund Burke once called "the permanent forces" in the community—the golden values to which people at their most high-minded might commit their loyalties and their energies.

Does what has been described by Christopher Lasch and others as a "narcissistic culture" imply that only fairly heroic types can lead the way in the "civilized treatment of others"? Nothing in the papers and in the panel discussion would lead to this conclusion. College and university presidents are chosen for their potential for leadership. But great leadership need not be Churchillian. A conveyed sense of commitment, courage, and fairness by average executives can usually compensate mightily for an absence of charisma. And in twilight crises of uncertainty, charisma itself can be counterproductive. Ever since Ichabod Crane, there has been something faintly sinister or ridiculous about academics on horseback.

If I have any quarrel with the essays and the ensuing discussion, it stems from a doubt that the future will be as lugubrious as assumed. It is true that the authors and panelists found reasons for guarded optimism. But these tend to be overshadowed by gloom. It may be legitimate to use my prefatory prerogatives to accent the positive. I do not wish to discount the dangers. We in this nation have ground out a lot of history in the past five or six decades— much of it sullen (wars, depressions, assignations, profligacies, inflations, metastatic technology). We are now caught up in an ebbtide of the great wave of faith in education and knowledge that hit its peak in the mid-1960s. But if we were then too buoyant, too sure, too optimistic, we are now too discouraged, too doubtful, too pessimistic. We should take pride and comfort in what has been learned in the past several years. Furthermore, there are new green shoots coming out of every nook and cranny, if we would only take pains to look carefully.

What of lasting value have we learned from the experiences of the past several decades?

First of all, we have learned that distant events have proximate effects. American presidents do not chase around to Vienna and Tokyo and Mexico City for the fun of it. They go to those exotic places because that is where the important action is—action that will mightily effect the health and well-being of Americans in every state and hamlet. Similarly, college and university administrators have increased their links to state capitals and to Washington a thousand-fold in the past twenty years. They have learned that what happens on campus is mightily affected by a hundred distant influences: court decisions, federal regulations, reporting requirements of state coordinating committees, NLRB rulings, state and federal tax laws, public referenda. They have learned that the protection of local options and autonomies is directly related to influencing influentials in distant settings.

This recognition of interrelatedness is the first cause

for optimism. Leaders of the academy are far less likely to be caught by Starwar surprises emanting from other political and administrative galaxies than they were a few years ago. If distant early-warning radar screens and political laser beams need further perfecting, at least there is a new and heartening recognition of the issue.

Second, with all of the tawdry complexity of modern bureaucratic life in education, some remarkable things have happened in the past three decades—developments in the moral climate of our nation that only the least generous among us could rue. The fact is that the hard shell of caste and class that had existed since colonial times in large parts of our nation has cracked beyond repair in the past quarter-century. However far we still have to go, minorities, women, the young, the old, the handicapped are finally being brought, in Winston Churchill's great words, "under the protective umbrella of the Constitution." This extraordinary happening—the explosive extension of the concept of fairness in our society—is fraught with unpredictable, uncomfortable, sometimes bizzare consequences. It affronts the comfortable, often-hidden, class system that in earlier days ensured that some people were more equal than others. But the recent transformation of expectations is a substantial moral triumph. It changes the definition of education from "sorting" to "universal opportunity." That the in-baskets of collegiate executives are loaded with clinical problems related to the implementation of the new equities should be viewed as a kind of midwifery. In the context of considerable pain, blood, and anguish, college and university administrators are helping a new world—a new freedom—to be born.

This seems to me a second cause for optimism—even

though the struggle will be sufficiently attenuated to dull on occasion the administrator's sense of immediate accomplishment.

Third, I cannot help but feel that we are coming to the end of a decade of educational slobbery. Standards are once again becoming respectable. The fakes are being spotlighted on "Sixty Minutes" and in books and journals. Whatever the perversities of decremental budgets—fewer real bucks next year than this—they can be used to separate the frivolous from the serious.

I refer here not just to the back-to-basics movement—basics defined in terms of the traditional three-Rs. There are, in fact, some very worrisome aspects to this movement. Unless we are careful, we may turn out graduates who have been trained to recognize words, memorize facts, manipulate numbers, and write a simple declarative sentence but who are incapable of a level of thought, feeling, and action needed for personal and social survival in the twenty-first century. The new concern with standards should infuse and infect *all* learning and *all* courses at *all* levels—in the arts and literature, in health and consumerism, in history and social studies, in science and language, in professional and technical training. I see within institutions of higher education, within state and federal authorities, and within private accrediting associations a new concern about the commitment to and the maintenance of academic standards.

There is a final point. I see a new emphasis on the need to equip college and university leaders with management skills necessary to the responsible fulfillment of their tasks. This volume commemorates the tenth anniversary of the Institute for Educational Management at Harvard. The thousand or so higher-education administrators who have enrolled in the summer Institute have contributed to the curriculum as they have learned from it. In graduate schools across the nation, a new sophistication is being brought to the process of educating future college and university administrators. In addition to stressing traditional management tools—quantitative and qualitative—new preservice and inservice curricula for college and university administrators are emphasizing the political and legal environment of higher education, organizational behavior, collective bargaining, and the purposes and effects of education. The graduates of these courses and programs should be far better educated than their predecessors in the leadership skills needed to guide a modern institution of higher education.

These, then, are reasons for considerable optimism as one views the future of college and university administration. This volume of essays and commentary rightly emphasizes the coming dangers and complexities. Reasons for hope are alluded to in what follows. They are simply underscored in this preface.

Stephen K. Bailey, Ph.D., is the Director of Programs in Administration, Planning, and Social Policy at Harvard's Graduate School of Education. The author of several books and articles, Professor Bailey is particularly known for his prize-winning study, **Congress Makes A Law,** *and for his most recent book,* **The Purposes of Education.**

Introduction

The evidence of demographic analysis is incontestable: enrollments for institutions of higher learning will decrease markedly in the 1980s. The most dramatic consequence of projected declines will be the contraction of finances of colleges and universities. Undoubtedly, the fiscal diminution will post the most central challenge to educational administrators in the decade ahead, demanding from them a synthesis of leadership and managerial behaviors that will address the evolutionary needs of the academy.

In the spring of 1979, the Institute for Educational Management conducted a Symposium on Leadership by which it hoped to discover guidelines for its role in developing and enhancing the leadership skills of administrators for the 1980s. Two papers were presented to generate discussion by the panelists of such guidelines, and both are included in this volume. "Educating Administrators and Professionals" by Chris Argyris and "Managing Universities in the 1980s by Richard M. Cyert have been prefaced by Stephen K. Bailey. Professor Bailey has written a preface in which he assesses the challenges to educational leadership in the past several decades, against which he poses an optimistic argument for the '80s.

Chris Argyris's essay, "Education Administrators and Professionals," goes to the heart of the decline of public confidence in institutions and professionals by elaborating the concepts of single- and double-loop learning. He proposes ways by which academic leaders may unfreeze the predisposition for the status quo that exists in single-loop learning in order to make way for double-loop detection and correction of error that involves the changing of underlying values and policies.

Richard M. Cyert's essay, "Managing Universities in the 1980s," focuses the major problem facing academic administrators in the following question, "How can the attention of faculties be kept focused on maintaining excellence in the face of forces pulling the attention to survival?" Uncertainty will prevail with regard to how institutions will reduce their scales of operation, and university presidents will be involved to a greater degree than in the past with conflict resolution at a level of individual problems. Cyert offers a host of strategies indicating how administrators may best manage the complex deescalation problems facing them.

"Leadership: An Attempt to Look at the Future" by Gene I. Maeroff, summarizes the essays and offers an analysis of the discussion by the symposium participants.

As Professor Bailey notes in his preface, the essays are complementary — presenting as they do both the theoretical side of the issue of leadership (Argyris) and the practically applied strategies of financial management (Cyert). Together, they offer a keen-sighted perspective on the central challenge to higher education in the decade about to unfold. It would be difficult to imagine a college or university administrator who was not assisted by the thinking expounded in these four responses to the difficulties of academic "leadership in the 1980s."

Educating Administrators and Professionals

by Chris Argyris

I begin with some puzzling facts. As the sophistication of managerial technology and competence increases, polls inform us that (1) the public's confidence in the ability of private and public organizations to perform effectively decreases (Argyris, 1973) and (2) the confidence of the public in professionals who provide services and manage institutions has steadily decreased. In many cases, including education, it is at an all-time low (National Opinion Research Corporation, 1978).

Since the technical knowledge used by these different professionals is so disparate, it appears unlikely that it can be the cause of the deteriorating confidence. We must look elsewhere for what is common to these professions that could cause these trends.

Common to administrators and all other professionals is that they require valid information to use their technical skills, that they must get this information from others, and frequently the people from whom they must get the information are also the people they must manage (either to produce a product or a service). Professionals have the difficult task of combining learning through others with controlling or managing these same others. This is a difficult task because the conditions required for learning may be, as we shall see, at odds with the conditions required for controlling or managing others.

To compound the problem, the new managerial technology appears to be most effective for detecting and correcting the more routine everyday errors. It is poorly suited to detect and correct the more fundamental errors in policies and assumptions and paradoxes, like the one just cited. To compound the problem even further, I hope to show that we acculturate people, at a very early age, with "theories of action" that are, at best, effective for correcting routine error and, at worst, counterproductive for ignoring the more fundamental errors. To compound the already over compounded, these people will necessarily create learning systems in organizations that sanction and reinforce the above so that framing the problem as changing these factors will appear to be, to any rational person, irrational and impractical.

These self-sealing processes, I also hope to show, are reinforced by present educational programs in most professional schools and by the research being conducted to inform professional practice and education.

Single- and double-loop learning

Learning is defined as detecting error (mismatch) or correcting it (match). Individuals can learn but so too can groups or organizations. The latter learn through individuals acting as agents of the group or organization.

I should like to highlight two types of learning. Single-loop learning is any detecting and correction of error that does not alter the underlying values or policies of the organization (or, for that matter, any unity). Changing class schedules or changing curriculi can be single-loop learning if the underlying governing values of the university's education purposes are not altered. Double-loop learning is any detection and correction of error that involves the changing of underlying values and policies. Single-loop learning focuses on changing the routines; double-loop learning focuses on changing the values and policies from which the routines are designed.

Returning to the puzzle with which I began, it will be my task in this paper to suggest that most sophisticated management technology is aimed at single-loop learning. The causes of citizen loss of confidence, however, are related more to double-loop issues—some of which make even single-loop learning unlikely.

I am not taking the position that single-loop learning is unimportant. The reason for creating organizations is to decompose problems into single-loop activities. Unless the routines are performed well, the organization will not be able to achieve even its most primitive obligations. All of us in academia have seen examples of bright scholars who organize to deal with double-loop issues only to have their organizations deteriorate because they could not solve simple single-loop problems.

My position, therefore, is that single-loop is necessary but not sufficient for several reasons. First, conditions may change and the original governing values and policies are no longer applicable. Single-loop learning will not help us to solve such problems.

Individuals are socialized to be single-loop learners and to create organizations with the same learning limitations.

Second, I hope to show that human beings also use a technology to design and execute their actions. This individual managerial technology is learned through acculturation. Research to date suggests that the managerial technology most frequently held by individuals limits them to single-loop learning and acts to blind them to this possibility. One consequence is that organizations are populated with single-loop learners who then create organizational conditions that reinforce and sanction this limitation.

It is correct, therefore, to describe the Pentagon Papers, the Firestone Tire fiasco, the Swine Flu program, the near financial collapse of large cities, and the failure of alternative schools as examples of poor organizational double-loop learning. It is incorrect, however, to place the blame primarily on organizations. They could not have done much better (even with the sophisticated information science technology) because they are populated by human beings who, for the most part, do not know how to double-loop learn—not to say how to create organizations that double-loop learn.

For example, five schools were studied whose teachers and students were volunteers, whose curricula were largely, if not completely, under their control, and who had adequate financial support. Yet they all failed. When one examines the reasons for the failure, they lie in the interpersonal, group, and intergroup dynamics that they created. The teachers and students were single-loop learners trying to establish schools that require double-loop skills (Argyris, 1974). Another example is, I believe, the rise and demise of faculty and student participation in university governance. According to recent evaluations, such participation has not been effective (Baldridge et al, 1978). If our knowledge about individual information processing, about the organizational learning systems, and about real time constraints is valid, then mechanisms such as university senates should have difficulty in dealing with double-loop issues. At best, they may be used for dealing with single-loop issues. As we shall see, if individuals and organizations have trouble in double-loop learning, one way to deal with the problem is to decompose the double-loop issues to single-loop ones. But, the reason they were created was because of factors such as low trust, organizational games, unilaterally made decisions that were uninfluenceable. These are double-loop issues that are not decomposable to single-loop issues.

Learning in order to understand, and learning in order to take action

Is this not an overly pessimistic view? Have not universities and professional schools been concerned with double-loop learning for years? Does not the core of many curricula include questioning the underlying governing values and policies of the society and of the respective professional discipline?

The answer is yes to both questions. But such an answer does not deal with the problem that I am raising. Why is this so?

Learning has been described as a circular process of *discovery* (of a problem), *invention* (of a solution), *production* (of the solution), and *evaluation* (of the production) which may lead to new discoveries. Most professional schools pay attention to the entire cycle when they are teaching knowledge for single-loop learning. For example, accounting is taught so that students learn to discover the conditions when LIFO and FIFO are valid and to apply the proper accounting procedure under the proper conditions. Students are taught decision analysis in ways that they can use for the solving of actual problems.

The knowledge and skills, however taught, that are related to double-loop learning, rarely include the entire cycle of learning. Inquiry into errors in the underlying policies and practices of organizations is taught in professional schools primarily at the level of discovery and, in fewer cases, at the level of invention. Little is taught about *producing* double-loop knowledge into action. For example, much is taught about such leadership skills as creating conditions for inquiry and trust, minimizing conformity, and reducing counterproductive bureaucratic games, but rarely do the students learn how to produce these skills under on-line conditions.

One very important consequence is that the students are left with a considerable gap between knowledge about the problem and the competence to produce a viable solution in an action context. This means that, at best, we have students who may understand the problem but do not know what to do about it. This is not a tragedy because administrators are often faced with gaps between knowledge and action. But few students are taught the skills of gap filling, especially for double-loop problems. There are therefore two levels of double-loop skills that are needed. The first is detection and correction of double-loop errors. The second is gap filling when one does not know how to accomplish the first.

To complicate matters, in some fields there is a third problem. The knowledge produced may vary more significantly if the discovery and invention are for the sake of discovery and invention than if they are for the sake of production. We frame different discoveries and different inventions when the purpose is to produce a solution in the everyday world than when the purpose is only to understand or to discover the everyday world. For example, Allison (1971) attempted to discover what happened in the decision-making processes during the Cuban Missile Crisis. Once Allison developed an adequate description, he showed that the three models of decision making and organization in good currency at that time provided valid but incomplete pictures of reality. Allison argued that all three were needed. He also invented suggestions for how to prevent some of the decision-making problems in the future.

There is almost nothing presented, however, about how to produce these inventions in real life. If this step is taken, important contradictions embedded in the advice may begin to surface. For example, the Cyert and March model (Allison's Level II) states that in most organizations coalitions exist that are continually at war with each other. These intergroup conflicts lead to such consequences as quasi-resolution of conflict and highly limited search (Cyert and March, 1963). Allison presented evidence to illustrate these features (Level III). Cyert and March and Allison, however, appear to accept these as given, as highly unlikely that anything will ever be done to change these features. This view is correct and it is self-sealing. It is correct in the sense that researchers using different theories document these features of organizational life. It is self-sealing because intergroup warfare and low trust not only create and reinforce quasi-resolution of conflict and limited search; they usually make it undiscussable. It is difficult to correct factors that are not discussable.

Baldridge's (1971) diagnosis of power and conflict in a large city university is detailed and thorough. But the inventions of how to overcome the problems are not only brief, they are abstract. Thus Baldridge recommends that university presidents should be seen as statesmen rather than as bureaucrats. He concludes that, "One of the most important practical implications emerging from this study is the importance of maintaining the decision network." How to do this? The answer is better communication, the development of a large back-up staff of experts, and the involvement of all significant interest groups and structural divisions in policies that affect them (pp. 206-207).

But how does one produce better communication and generate genuine involvement? This advice has been given for decades, but few leaders are able to produce it.

Moreover, the advice can reinforce old problems of the university and create new ones. For example, we now have ample evidence that a large back-up staff of experts can create new and deeper divisions within an organization. I would also predict that there are situations where the back-up staff of experts can create new and deeper divisions within an organization. I would also predict that there are situations where the back-up staffs are comparable in size and competence yet the resolution of conflict differs significantly. We also have evidence that providing people with an opportunity to participate in decisions that involve them may be counterproductive and may not even be appreciated by the people we are trying to involve (Baldridge et al, 1978).

A counterresponse is that such factors as quasi-resolution of conflict and limited search are due to the finite information capacities of individuals and not the Level III factors that I describe. This response is not counter to the argument. For example, Simon (1969) indicates that the individual's finite information-processing capacities can be extended by the use of external memories. Other individuals and groups can serve this purpose. But in order to do so, they must have a relationship with the individual that is one of trying to be of genuine help and to provide valid information. Moreover, theories-in-use and learning systems can determine which conflicts among competing coalitions will be and will not be explored thoroughly.

Espoused theory and theory-in-use

There is another problem not faced up to adequately in most professional education. It may be described as the difference between the theories people espouse and those they actually use in an action context.

Recent research by Donald Schon and myself suggests that people have theories of action, in their heads about how to design and implement intended consequences. Initially, we thought that if we understood people's theories of action we should be able to predict their actions (actions are behaviors with meanings). This hypothesis assumed that if people had theories about how and what actions to design, they would use them *and* that people could not design actions that were not derivable from their theories.

These assumptions turned out to be correct, but for reasons that were much more complicated than we had originally imagined. First, we inferred individuals' theories of action by interviewing them. But we found that when we observed them, they did not behave according to the theories that they had described. So we kept the original idea that people have theories of action in their heads but dropped the idea that they could describe them accurately. We called the theories of action that they reported their espoused theories.

Next we took the observations and tape recordings that we made and inferred the theory that the actors must have used (if there was a connection between maps in peoples' heads and their actions). We called that theory their theory-in-use. We found that with the theory-in-use we could make accurate predictions (or more accurately, our predictions were not disconfirmed) about present and future actions, that many of our predictions were counter to those made by the actions, that our predictions came out right even when the actors knew about them and did not wish them to be confirmed (Argyris, 1976a, 1976b).

We concluded that we had a powerful concept, but one that required some bewildering assumptions about human beings. We were not simply saying that people did not behave according to their espoused theories. We were saying that people had theories in their heads that informed their actions, about which they were unaware, and over which they therefore had little conscious control. If they did not have control over their theories-in-use, then in what sense were they in control over the design and execution of their actions?

Another consistent finding was that although people would give us the "wrong" in-use theory, they readily agreed with our formulation of their theory-in-use. Why such blindness and quick agreement? After all, the theory-in-use was inferred from the relatively directly observable behavior such as tape recordings of conversations. They had access to their directly observable behavior.

The blindness and yet quick agreement to which we are referring is a puzzling finding. We are only just beginning to understand it. We know from others' research that human beings are finite information-processing systems and that their immediate or on-line span of attention may be limited (Miller, 1956; Simon, 1969). People learn complex actions by decomposing them and going through much practice and iterative learning. Once the actions become skilled, they become second nature or tacit. Indeed, the only way the actions can be skillfully performed is to do them without thinking. But to do them without thinking makes it highly unlikely that there will be conscious awareness of what one is doing or saying. However, once the actions have been produced, then the individuals may reflect on them.

Model I theories-in-use

We are also learning about the way we pay attention to different factors when we are in an action mode and when we are in an inquiry mode. It appears that most people hold theories-in-use that make it highly unlikely they will seek to combine action with inquiry. How do we arrive at these conclusions?

Most people hold a theory-in-use that we call Model I (see Exhibit I). One central proposition in that theory is, "Advocate your position as clearly as you can, and couple it with unilaterally controlling others in order to win." Another is, "Unilaterally and covertly censor information in order to save others and your own face." A third is, "Minimize the creation of situations that may produce feelings, especially negative ones."

If we behave this way toward others, then they may feel, for example, persuaded, coerced, or manipulated. But given the second proposition of Model I, the one action that we are unlikely to take is to make our feelings of coercion and manipulation discussable. We, too, will then go into action with our response, which also will be to advocate and try to win. This, in turn, will have the negative conse-

Exhibit I
Theories of action

Governing variables for action	Action strategies for actor	Consequences on actor and his associates	Consequences on learning	Effectiveness
I	II	III	IV	V
Model I				
1 Achieve the purposes as I perceive them.	1 Design and manage environment so that actor is in control over factors relevant to me.	1 Actor seen as defensive.	1 Self-sealing.	
2 Maximize winning and minimize losing.	2 Own and control task.	2 Defensive interpersonal and group relationships.	2 Single loop learning.	Decreased.
3 Minimize eliciting negative feelings.	3 Unilaterally protect self.	3 Defensive norms.	3 Little testing of theories publicly.	
4 Be rational and minimize emotionality.	4 Unilaterally protect others from being hurt.	4 Low freedom of choice, internal commitment, and risk taking.		
Model II				
1 Valid information.	1 Design situations or encounters where participants can be origins and experience high personal causation.	1 Actor seen as minimally defensive.	1 Testable processes.	
2 Free and informed choice.	2 Task is controlled jointly.	2 Minimally defensive interpersonal relations and group dynamics.	2 Double loop learning.	Increased.
3 Internal commitment to the choice and constant monitoring of the implementation.	3 Protection of self is a joint enterprise and oriented toward growth.	3 Learning-oriented norms.	3 Frequent testing of theories publicly.	
	4 Bilateral protection of others.	4 High freedom of choice, internal commitment, and risk taking.		

Note: *Exhibit I* taken from Chris Argyris and Donald Schon, *Theory in Practice* (San Francisco: Jossey-Bass, 1974.)

quences on the others that they had on us when they were behaving in a Model I fashion.

Hence professional schools may espouse administrative leadership that encourages organizational double-loop learning. However, it is our prediction that the students are

13

not capable of creating such conditions and that they are unaware that this is the case. Moreover, once they become aware, the insight does not lead to the acquisition of the skills for double-loop learning.

Professional schools are going to have to face the fact that unfreezing Model I theories-in-use that are learned through acculturation (it appears that twelve-year old children are competent with Model I) requires at least as much effort and attention as is required to teach the more complicated quantitative managerial technology. I am also saying that unless administrators learn these new skills, they will rarely create organizations that double-loop learn.

Organizational Learning Systems

I stated above that people can only design actions that are consonant with their theories-in-use. Organizations, however, are initially designed from rational models about how to decompose problems into manageable tasks and then to coordinate these tasks in order to achieve the intended consequences. These are the designs that lead to various shapes of pyramidal structures. Pyramidal structures are essentially theories of job specialization and coordination through hierarchical control. They contain an implicit theory of learning which is that if people observe errors, they will either correct them or report them to others to correct them.

There are at least two difficulties with this theory of

learning. First, it is intimately related to the theory of hierarchical control. Hence, people may fear detecting error if it could mean their job. Second, in the case of double-loop learning, they have fears that go beyond job survival. They have doubts about their ability to surface problems that might be threatening without creating interpersonal rejection and hostility.

Some administrators may wish that this were not the case. Some may even plead with their people that they be candid. A few may even try to create greater freedom to be candid by redesigning the theory of control. These steps, noble as they are, will be limited in effectiveness because people do not have the skills to deal with the probably personal negative consequences on self and others.

Moreover, people create in all organizations a system of norms, rules, procedures, and policies about the detection and the correction of error. These "learning systems" appear so far to be consonant with the constraints of Model I (see Exhibit II). Model O-I learning systems tend to make deviants out of employees who blow the whistle on threatening issues or who wish to surface organizational games that are undiscussable. At this point, individuals need no longer look at their personal responsibility for inhibiting double-loop learning (due to their Model I theory-in-use). The individuals can point to the organizational learning system embedded in a theory of unilateral hierarchical control as the "culprits."

Finally, a society full of organizations with O-I learning systems will necessarily have a limited capacity to regulate them. Regulating agencies, according to this perspective, have all the problems of organizational learning described above. Yet they are supposed to monitor other organiza-

Exhibit II
Model 0-1: Learning systems that inhibit error detection and correction

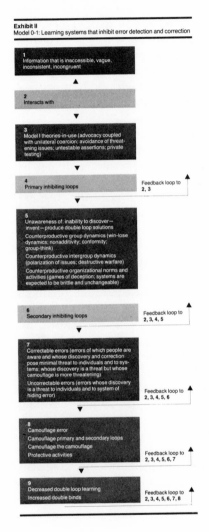

1 Information that is inaccessible, vague, inconsistent, incongruent

2 Interacts with

3 Model I theories-in-use (advocacy coupled with unilateral coercion; avoidance of threatening issues; untestable assertions; private testing)

4 Primary inhibiting loops — Feedback loop to 2, 3

5 Unawareness of; inability to discover—invent—produce double loop solutions
Counterproductive group dynamics (win-lose dynamics; nonadditivity; conformity; group-think)
Counterproductive intergroup dynamics (polarization of issues; destructive warfare)
Counterproductive organizational norms and activities (games of deception; systems are expected to be brittle and unchangeable)

6 Secondary inhibiting loops — Feedback loop to 2, 3, 4, 5

7 Correctable errors (errors of which people are aware and whose discovery and correction pose minimal threat to individuals and to systems; whose discovery is a threat but whose camouflage is more threatening)
Uncorrectable errors (errors whose discovery is a threat to individuals and to system of hiding error) — Feedback loop to 2, 3, 4, 5, 6

8 Camouflage error
Camouflage primary and secondary loops
Camouflage the camouflage
Protective activities — Feedback loop to 2, 3, 4, 5, 6, 7

9 Decreased double loop learning
Increased double binds — Feedback loop to 2, 3, 4, 5, 6, 7, 8

tions. If this is the case, then we may predict that regulating the regulated organizations will tend (1) to create interorganizational relationships that are consistent with their respective O-I learning systems, (2) to be blind to their respective inabilities to double-loop learn and hence (3) to strive, in the long run, to translate or reduce double-loop problems into single-loop problems.

It is my position that neither the double-loop problems within or among organizations will be corrected unless the professionals are educated to detect and correct double-loop errors and to create organizational learning systems that encourage such learning. Unfortunately, there is a dearth of information on how to diagnose organizations' capacities for double-loop learning. There is even less on how to enhance these abilities.

The role of research in producing knowledge related to double-loop learning

Many of the organizational and administrative theories stemming from social psychology (1969, 1975), sociology (1972), behavioral theories of the firm (1973), and public administration (1976) appear to focus primarily on producing advice that remains within Models I and O-I. Hence it is not relevant to double-loop learning.

This does not mean that scholars do not espouse double-loop ideas. Indeed, much of the research examined in the searches above was designed to raise double-loop issues. The advice that the researchers derived from their theories for the administrators, however, was primarily single-loop. For example, researchers who were interested in building trust recommended actions that also encouraged mistrust. Researchers who were against unilateral manipulative governmental theories-in-use during the Vietnam War advised young people to use the same theories-in-use when they tried to overcome these injustices (Argyris, 1975).

The cause for the single-loop or status quo feature of social science is first due, I suggest, to a fundamental tenet embedded in the practice of social science research. If the objective of social science is to describe the world as it is and if the world is basically Models I and O-I, then it should come as no surprise that the results of such research remain within the constraints of Models I and O-I (Argyris, 1979). For example, it is not surprising to read that researchers studying leadership in universities say that they assume it is highly unlikely that anyone will ever create a world of organizations significantly different from the present one (Cohen and March, 1974). The difficulty with this statement, again, is not that it is false; it is that it is a self-fulfilling prophecy.

Under these conditions an innovative research contribution is one that (1) describes the world as it is and does so more rigorously than previous attempts and (2) explains more than previously explained and (3) presents some counterintuitive findings. Cohen and March (1974) have made such an innovative contribution in their garbage-can theory of decision making. The theory represents a more elegant discovery.

But the difficulty with such research becomes apparent when we take seriously the consequences for action that flow from it. The theory of administrative leadership that March derives from their perspective is, to use his label, a "mini-Machiavellian" theory. The very title acknowledges that the action implications are Model I and have been for centuries. Here is an interesting puzzle. Research that describes the world differently and innovatively leads to action recommendations that are not new. I believe one explanation for the puzzle is that the new perspective is a new perspective of the same old world. As long as the perspective is valid, it will remain within the constraints of the present world. Again, there is nothing wrong with this as a description of reality. The question is related to what is our responsibility in conducting research that goes beyond these propositions that maintain the status quo.

To compound the difficulties created by limiting social science to being descriptive is the possibility that the theory-in-use for carrying out rigorous research is congruent with Model I and leads to O-I conditions. I have indicated above that due to individual theories-in-use and learning systems, there is a systematic blindness on the part of people related to double-loop issues and they are unaware of the blindness. If so, then studying the world as it is with the use of methods that are consonant to that world, it becomes highly unlikely that researchers will discover what their subjects are unaware of and how the societal learning systems act to make sure this is the case.

There is a way to discover the factors that are largely hidden from us. The method is based on realization that all the actions that are counterproductive to double-loop learning are skillful. Skillful actions are based, as we have seen, on tacit programs that produce automatic responses which, in this case, are reinforced by society.

The method required is to interrupt the skills by making them unskillful. This means that we must place people in learning environments that are different from the ones in which they presently exist. But this is not likely to occur if the goal of research and if the technology of research combine to remain within the requirements of Models I and O-I.

Social scientists must develop, therefore, models of alternative universes that do not presently exist. It is by comparing the conditions of the present universe with other possible universes that the predisposition for the status quo will be unfrozen. Unless researchers are able to surface and explain what is now unsurfaceable, they will not be achieving their present avowed purpose—namely, to understand and explain the universe as accurately and as comprehensively as possible.

Research that remains within the status quo may have far-reaching consequences for what is judged to be sound practical advice. For example, Neustadt and Fineberg (1978) published a diagnosis of the decision-making processes around the Swine Flu Program. They have organized a mass of data in an informative and systematic picture of what happened at the upper levels of management.

They also identify seven causal factors, six of which may be described as behavioral. They include (1) overconfidence by specialists in not fully validated theories about influenza and influenza epidemics, (2) actors advocating ideas based on personal agendas and acting as if this were not the case, and (3) subordinates manipulating superiors to perform as the former believed was correct. These factors are illustrative of people programmed with Model I and embedded in an O-I learning system.

When the authors turn to recommending ways of overcoming these problems, they suggest (1) requiring the actors to trace out the relationships between deadlines and each decision, (2) making explicit the assumptions underlying each decision, (3) developing awareness of tactics that polarize issues unnecessarily and inaccurately, and (4) forcing systematic and detailed airing of views on each question, one by one (pp. 87-89).

The relationship between the recommendations and the causes implies an assumption that administrators cannot deal directly with "overconfidence by specialists," "polarizing actions," "manipulating of superiors." This assumption is a valid one in a Model I world: it also acts to reinforce self-sealing processes. The fundamental thrust of the recommendations is to control or reduce error by tightening up the logic used by the actors and by making it subject to public inquiry. This thrust will work partially, and hence progress will be made. But when the information to be given is threatening, the actors will still find it necessary to polarize, oversell, and pressure. But now they will camouflage these actions even more in order to reduce the likelihood that they will be confronted.

There is another even more disturbing consequence. I have found few people whose camouflage works as well as they think it does. The recipients of the overselling and careful pressuring know what is going on. They may respond by (1) keeping their awareness secret, (2) discounting covertly what the others are saying, (3) excluding the others from certain meetings, or (4) unexplainably reducing their contact with them. They simultaneously camouflage their intentions. So we have a world increasingly "polluted" with games and camouflages that are undiscussable, and their undiscussability is undiscussable.

Perhaps the pollution has not reached the saturation point where the next game becomes the straw that breaks the camel's back. But, as in the case with air pollution in our cities, it is simply a matter of time.

I am recommending that professional schools take the lead in studying these pollution processes in order to reduce them. If we do not begin to take action, the ultimate loser will be the citizenry (especially those in underprivileged situations) and the professionals. The citizen may lose because it may be only corporations and governmental bureaus that can use their internal lawyers to check on the logic and assumptions of the external lawyers. As Bellow and Kettleson (1978) have shown, the poor may be able to sense that they are being pressured or manipulated, but they neither have the expertise nor the interpersonal skills to do much about it. As to the professionals, I believe it is these pollution issues more than the technical competence that are causing the decrease in confidence described at the outset.

Theories of instruction embedded in professional education: examples from experiential learning and the case method

So far I have tried to show how individual theories-in-use and systemic learning systems combine to make double-loop learning (at the individual or organizational levels) highly unlikely. Most of the present rigorous re-

22

rsity and company
ied the purposes of
the executives new
cobwebs" and (2) to
nity to meet and get
many different set-

The question being
objectives to help
erences among their
eir theories-in-use,
rning systems they
earn theories-in-use
d (4) to develop the

ptions of leader-

lls and the theories-
For example, Saario
taught such skills as:
lish and maintain a

al with subordinates
power, and depen-

ility to mediate con-

search maintains its rigor by following a theory-in-use that assures the production of knowledge to enhance single-loop learning and to reinforce the status quo.

It should not be surprising, therefore, if I conclude that professional education—*as it is practiced*, not espoused—reinforces the above loops against double-loop learning (again at the level of designing and implementing actions).

I believe it is self-evident that lectures and seminars controlled by faculty may espouse double-loop ideas because the theory-in-use of the learning context is Model I. I also believe that most of the ideas taught in professional schools intended to be implemented are single-loop ideas (e.g., LIFO or FIFO, management by objectives, decision theory, and PPBS).

There are two types of learning environments where double-loop learning has been tried. The first is the case method, and the second is the various forms of experiential learning such as T-groups.

Elsewhere, I have tried to show that experiential learning, in general, and T-groups in particular, developed limits for double-loop learning because they committed the same fundamental error as did those methods of learning based on Model I. T-group staffs tended to act as if the way to deal with the polarization against feelings was to polarize against rationality and cognition (Argyris, 1967; Back, 1972). Also, if most traditional education focused on discovery of ideas, T-groups focused on discovery of feelings. Both intended that the insights lead to a better world, i.e., a world that manifested less counterproductive forces to learning. Yet neither focused adequately on the skills necessary to produce the double-loop learning if the world was to be rid of some of its counterproductive forces.

Model I theories of administration err in the neg
what hierarchies can do to people (e.g., by placing t
dependent, submissive situations and in many case
forming nonchallenging tasks). Experiential theorie
ministration ignored the paradox that one reaso
humane" hierarchies are created is the humane fea
individuals—namely, their finite information-pro
capacity.

The latter limitation has a profound impact
probabilities that participation will be effective. If
have finite information-processing limits, then there
a limit to how much variance in information they ca
and act on. But if our view is correct, Models I and
combine to raise the probability for error (especially
to double-loop issues) by several magnitudes.

This is not to say that participation and power
tion were not useful ideas. It is to say that their lim
not systematically explored. Again, this is simila
blinders exhibited by those who generate Model I
ogy. For example, program planning and budgeti
much-needed technology, but it had embedded i
tations that were rarely acknowledged by its desig
relate this to our theoretical perspective, we have f
Model I theories-in-use and those that are the of
Model I lead to different but equally counterpi
paths to double-loop learning (Argyris, 1972, 19

Let us now turn to the case method. Rec
observed and tape recorded all the case sessions
executive program (Argyris, 1979). The analysis
recordings indicates that although faculty espouse
ing environment where students participated h
student-teacher dependence was kept at minimal

troubled the directors of severa
executive programs. All of them
their program to be (1) to introd
ideas "to unfreeze" or "blow away
provide the executives with an of
to know other high-level executi
tings.

These objectives are not tr
asked is how we may go beyond
executives (1) become aware of th
exposed theories, their actions,
(2) become aware of the kinds
create in their organizations, (3)
that facilitate double-loop learnin
skills to implement these new id

The limitations of present c
ship and managerial techno

The first step is to define the
in-use with which to implement th
(1979) suggests that administrators
• Peer skills: the ability to e
network of contacts with equals.
• Leadership skills: the ability t
and the complications of authori
dence.
• Conflict resolution skills: the

flict, handle disturbances, and work under psychological stress.

• Information-processing skills: the ability to build networks, extract and validate information, and disseminate information effectively (p. 344).

Definitions such as these are not adequate for several reasons. First, administrators must take action. Hence, the abilities to establish and maintain effective networks, to deal with the complications of authority, power, and dependence must be translated into action. Saario, I believe, would respond that this is obvious, that this connection must be made. What is not obvious, and we come to the second reason for the inadequacy, is that the gap between specifying these abilities and producing them under on-line constraints is very wide, and the actors are rarely aware of this fact when they are under on-line constraints. Hence, third, most administrators will design and implement actions consonant with Model I, which means, as we have seen, that the actions will be counterproductive to the competences just cited. Fourth, the consequences combine to make it highly likely that these lists can be used to maintain the status quo. For example, if one deals with coalition groups the way Lyndon Johnson did (a recommendation that Saario makes) the result should be a reinforcement of the dysfunctional aspects that create many of the coalition problems in the first place. People programmed with Model I theories-in-use have the skills "to build networks, extract and validate information, and disseminate information" for single-loop issues but not for double-loop issues. When people are faced with double-loop problems and the information available tends to be ambiguous, unclear, inconsistent, or incongruent, the tendency will be to problem-solve in ways that will make the information more ambiguous, unclear, inconsistent, and incongruent.

The second step is to realize that most of the managerial technology involved has embedded in it theories of learning and control that are congruent with Model I. The theory of learning embedded in the present managerial technology (such as decision analysis and management information systems) is that if people are required to make their reasoning more explicit and public, the inconsistencies, incongruities, ambiguities will be surfaced for at least two reasons. First, people will surface others' inconsistencies, incongruities, and ambiguities if someone else can be held responsible for their doing so. They can maintain, "I did not wish to get you in trouble, I had to do it." Second, people will surface their own inconsistencies, incongruities, and ambiguities to the extent that the managerial technology requires them to make their reasoning public. The first belief assumes that the predisposition created by theories-in-use and organizational learning systems can be bypassed or muted if the top (through their managerial technology) can be held responsible for surfacing the hitherto not surfaceable and making it discussable. The second belief assumes that people prefer to become aware of their inconsistencies and that such awareness will not have a negative effect on their future predispositions to discover error. Both of these assumptions are questionable, especially in a Model I world.

Features of new learning environments for educating administrators and other professionals

Understanding one's theory-in-use and organizational learning system requires beginning with relatively directly observable data because these phenomena are inferred from peoples' actions, not simply from what they report. This means that somehow in our classrooms we will have to introduce more relatively directly observable data than is presently the case. This requirement is not too difficult to fulfill in the schools that use the case method. As we have shown above, if people are given a chance to become involved in actual cases, they will expose their Model I behavior and soon create an O-I learning system within the classroom. What is needed is a faculty member who is able to help students reflect on their actions produced during the class.

Much research is needed before we know the most efficient ways to accomplish this objective. One possible mode is to have the students participate in a module that focuses heavily on teaching a theory of action perspective. That module would overlap with a case study class, let us say, on policy analysis, or strategic planning, or marketing strategy. The latter sessions would be tape recorded. The faculty could draw samples from the tapes to be discussed in the theory of action module. It is possible to help students see how they are competing, evaluating, not listening, or playing games. It is also possible to show that when they are helped to role-play many of their recommendations for the action to take in the case, they produce these recommendations with competitiveness, unilateral evaluations, and win/lose dynamics. Thus it is possible to relate the analyses of the case by the students and their recommendations for action to the internal dynamics of the classroom.

As the students become more competent in this one-line reflection and analysis, it can be tried in the "substantive" class. One important requirement for the success of this learning environment is the relationship between the two instructors. On the one hand, it is important for the "substantive" faculty members to be accepting of their predisposition to behave in accordance with Model I. The operational definition for accepting is that the instructors are confrontable; that is, their actions toward the students are discussable. The "theory of action" instructor, on the other hand, has to be accepting of the limits placed on "process" by real time constraints and the requirements of achieving organizational objectives.

It is conceivable that the school may even make a service available to its students to tape-record their actions in any course in which they are heavily involved. For example, a student may be responsible for beginning the discussion in a finance course, and he would like to reflect on his behavior. Or a small group may have to make a presentation in a larger session.

A different model is to create a learning environment for a group of executives who are strangers to each other or for an executive and his immediate subordinates. The cases used in the class are developed by the executives. Some of the cases are written, while others are based on tape recordings sent to us by the executives of sessions that they led in their organizations. In the case of the latter, we listened to the tapes and transcribed a portion of them to be used as a case.

The results have been encouraging. The executives soon desire to introduce the learning in the back-home setting. This means that, in a class of ten, if five executives wish to begin, the teaching possibilities become significantly enlarged. Instead of one learning environment, ten are now required. The logistics are difficult but not unsolvable. One feature that helps is that the scheduling can be done a year ahead of time. We have found that the organizations are willing to commit financial resources to help guarantee a faculty for two years or more. Moreover, many clients have also been willing to make research opportunities available including paying for most of the cost. Their interest in research is related to their need to assess how well they are doing and to redesign the programs to reduce error and inefficiency (Argyris, 1976b).

A third type of learning environment is classes that focus on what I have called inner contradictions of management. These classes may be more advanced and may require exposure first to the learning environments just described. The purpose of these programs is to explore the deepest paradoxes that administrators face. For example, the people in decision theory and operations research have developed various systematic and formal models for managerial decision making. These models vary widely, but for the purposes of this discussion let us include them under the label of management information systems (MIS). The underlying assumption of this technology may be described as follows. Organizations contain many different "contexts of action" along the work flow. People close to the flow of work (teachers in a classroom and first-line supervisors in a

31

private or public organization) tend to manage their context with a personal MIS. The information used tends to be subjective, concrete, emotionally laden, nonadditive to and noncomparable with other personal MIS.

It is not possible for the president or dean of a university, or the president or assistant secretary, to manage their respective organizations with such MIS. It is at this level that operations research and decision theorists have been of help. They have developed MIS whose data may be described as abstract, impersonal, additive, trendable, and comparable, and whose logic is explicit. This is the kind of data that administrators, who are distant from the context of action, can use to manage the organization.

What will happen if these features dominate the reasoning processes at the top and hence dominate the major problem-solving and decision-making processes of organizations? It appears likely that end results may be emphasized over processes, and decisions can become distorted because the requirements of the information science technology may require reasoning processes that are reductionistic. This means that any discontinuous attributes are treated as simply involving "qualitative constraint" or denying or overlooking the existence of the discontinuity, which, in turn, may misstate the underlying structure and again, in turn, may anesthetize moral feeling (Tribe, 1972).

It also appears that the simultaneous use of distant and local information systems to administer organizations can lead managers at the local level or at the point where action is taken to feel that their world is managed unjustly. Since this would be a double-loop issue, they would also feel that the issue of "structural-based" injustice is undiscussable (Argyris, 1978). Faculty, for example, do not believe it is just to evaluate their performance by the use of distant data.

But they also believe that they must be careful of how they resist because they could be seen as troublemakers or disloyal. All these are threatening issues and require a climate of double-loop learning—a climate that we suggest rarely exists.

The result is a contradiction. If we decide to use rational information to manage organizations, we can create the conditions of irrationality and injustice which, in turn, may influence the validity of the information that may be collected in the first place.

A task of professional education of the future will be to help administrators to see that this contradiction cannot be eliminated. Distant information systems are needed, and irrationality and feelings of injustice are inevitable. The task is not only to redesign MIS or to re-educate people. Administrators and followers will have to be educated in dealing with paradoxes. If there is a requirement that is greatly underestimated in administrative education, it is this one. All too frequently, education is based on the assumption that dilemmas and paradoxes can be reduced or eliminated; the trick is to pick the right horn of the dilemma. This is a trick. The real challenge is to face the paradox and learn how to manage it.

Summary and Conclusions

I should like to conclude by summarizing the position taken in this paper as follows:

(1) Professionals, be they administrators or individual

33

contributors such as lawyers, doctors, educators, and clergy, have technical expertise that they use to accomplish their respective purposes.

(2) In order to use this knowledge, they must first "know" it. What does "to know" mean? Professionals know the knowledge when they can use it (a) to discover problems, (b) to invent a solution, (c) to produce the solution, (d) to evaluate how well they are doing, and (e) to perform a, b, c, and d in an on-line manner. To know is indeed very complex.

(3) We have found in our studies that professionals (all people, for that matter) are not particularly effective in on-line learning about double-loop issues.

They appear (a) to combine advocacy with unilateral control, or (b) to use oscillating Model I, or (c) the opposite to Model I (nondirective), or (d) oscillating between nondirective and unilaterally controlling.

(4) It is likely that the mistrust of and lack of confidence in professionals may be generated while the professionals and their clients are interacting. In the case of the professionals, they may unrealizingly act in ways that induce error.

For example, white, middle-class lawyers may behave in ways that lead black and disadvantaged clients to wonder if the lawyers understand blacks and, hence, if they are to be trusted. Subordinates may learn to conform to the requirements of the superior and to design games to hide the conformity because the superior espouses that subordinates should take initiative and be wild ducks. They may also camouflage the games. Moreover, if the setting is threatening, the subordinates may even camouflage the camouflage. Young parishioners may interpret attempts by clergy to give them insight into their emotional problems as evidence that they do not understand them.

34

Subordinates or clients utilizing Model I and remaining within the requirements of O-I learning systems will tend to assume that these kinds of problems are undiscussable. If the superiors (or professionals) are unaware of these assumptions, then, indeed, the assumed undiscussability becomes a self-fulfilling prophecy.

(5) One of the major tasks is to help professionals learn to use their technical knowledge and simultaneously reflect in an on-line mode on their practice. This means that they should learn the skills of taking action and encouraging inquiry into their action.

This is a difficult learning objective because most people use Model I, which means that they try to learn through the use of a theory of unilateral control (a theory counterproductive to double-loop learning) *and* to be unaware of this fact.

(6) The unawareness is less related to unconscious factors and much more related to the facts that:

(a) People are skilled at unilateral control. Skilled actions are accomplished through programs that are tacit. Hence the unawareness of the consequences is a necessary condition for producing the skill.

(b) Learning systems in most social systems encourage people in the name of caring, decency, and being civilized not to tell others when they are producing major errors that they appear to be unaware of.

(7) The major educational methods presently in use may be adequate to teach technical single- and perhaps double-loop ideas at the espoused level. Students tend "to know" double-loop ideas in the sense that they can use them to discover problems and, in some cases, to invent solutions. Few students are taught how to produce these solutions. The situation is even more bleak with respect to

interpersonal issues. Students may learn to discover and even, in some cases, invent solutions, but these competences are related primarily to the behavior of others. Rarely do students learn to discover, invent, and produce double-loop learning when they are personally involved. And even more rarely do they learn to do it while they are simultaneously trying to introduce double-loop learning around technical issues (such as financial analyses, cutting budgets, and reviving outmoded departments).

(8) Finally, much of the rigorous research being conducted that may have relevance to these issues is designed and implemented in ways that make it highly likely that the products will be most useful and powerful in maintaining the status quo.

Theories-in-use, learning systems, modes of education, and research relevant to leadership and professional practice appear to dovetail in ways that make individual and organizational double-loop learning unlikely. At the same time the very success of our society means that the next class of issues that will dominate the scene will be the inner contradictions and paradoxes embedded in organizations and professional practice. These issues require double-loop learning.

*Chris Argyris, Ph.D., is the James Bryant Conant Professor of Education and Organizational Behavior at Harvard University. The author of twenty-one books and monographs, including **Increasing Leadership Effectiveness**, Professor Argyris has been a special consultant to the U.S. Department of Health, Education, and Welfare and to numerous European governments on problems of executive development and productivity.*

Bibliography

Allison, Graham, *Essence of Decision* (New York: Little Brown & Co., 1971).

Argyris, Chris, "Inner Contradictions of Rigorous Research," (Manuscript) 1979.

Argyris, Chris, "Theories of Action that Inhibit Individual Learning," *American Psychologist*, Vol. 31, No. 9, September 1976a.

Argyris, Chris, *Increasing Leadership Effectiveness* (New York: Wiley-Interscience, 1976b).

Argyris, Chris, "Dangers in Applying Results from Experimental Social Psychology," *American Psychologist*, Vol. 30, No. 4, 1975, pp. 469-485.

Argyris, Chris, "Alternative Schools: A Behavioral Analysis," *Teachers College Record*, Vol. 75, No. 4, May 1974.

Argyris, Chris, "On Organizations of the Future" (New York: Russell Sage Foundation, 1973).

Argyris, Chris, *Management and Organization Development* (New York: McGraw-Hill, 1971).

Argyris, Chris and Donald Schon, *Organizational Learning* (Reading, Mass.: Addison-Wesley, 1978).

Argyris, Chris and Donald Schon, *Theory in Practice* (San Francisco, Calif.: Jossey-Bass, 1974).

Back, Kurt, *Beyond Words: The Story of Sensitivity Training and the Encounter Movement* (New York: Russell Sage Foundation, 1972).

Baldridge, J. Victor, David V. Curtis, George Ecker, and Gary L. Riley, *Policy Making and Effective Leadership* (San Francisco: Jossey-Bass, 1978).

Bellow, Gary and Jeanne Kettleson, "From Ethics to Politics: Confronting Scarcity and Fairness in Public Interest Practice," *Boston University Law Review*, Vol. 58, No. 3, May 1978.

Cohen, Michael D. and James G. March, *Leadership and Ambiguity, The American College President* (New York: McGraw-Hill, 1974).

Cyert, Richard M. and James G. March, *A Behavior Theory of the Firm* (Englewood Cliffs, N.J.: Prentice-Hall, Inc., 1963).

Miller, George, "The Magical Number Seven, Plus or Minus Two: Some Limits on Our Capacity for Processing Information," *Psychological Review*, Vol. 6, No. 3, pp. 81-97, 1956.

National Opinion Research Center, University of Chicago, *General Social Survey*, July 1978.

Neustadt, Richard and Harvey V. Fineberg, *The Swine Flu Affair*, U.S. Dept. of Health, Education and Welfare, 1978.

Saario, Terry Tinson, "Leadership and the Change Process: Preparing Educational Administrators," in (eds.) Robert E. Herriott and Neal Gross, *The Dynamics of Planned Educational Change* (McCutchan, 1979, pp. 328-350).

Simon, Herbert A., *The Sciences of the Artificial* (Cambridge, Mass.: MIT Press, 1969).

Tribe, Laurence H., "Policy Science: Analysis or Ideology," *Philosophy and Public Affairs*, Vol. 2, No. 1, 1972, pp. 66-110.

Argyris, Chris, "Executive Programs and Organizational Development," mimeographed, Harvard University, 1979.

Managing Universities in the 1980s

by Richard M. Cyert

Introduction

The problems of managing universities in the 1980s are going to be, in part, a function of the type and location of the institution. The problems are going to be different for public and private institutions. Small, private liberal arts colleges in areas of declining populations are going to have different problems from well-endowed universities with national reputations. Unisex schools will have difficulties that will be distinct from coed schools. Schools in rural locations will have to be managed differently from schools in urban areas. The distinctions could be further enumerated, but the point is clear. Colleges and universities like other organizations have different characteristics, and the effect of changes in the environment will not be the same for all institutions of higher learning.

Nevertheless, there are some problems that are general and some forces that will affect all education institutions. In particular, those problems generated by demographic changes will affect the whole society. The most overwhelming influence on educational institutions in the 1980s is the reduction in the number of high school graduates in the coming decade.

Decline in high school graduates

All people concerned with managing institutions of higher education are aware of the fact that the pool of students available for college will be declining markedly in the 1980s. Table I shows the number of high school graduates from 1970 to 1986. Obviously, the figures for the 1980s are projections. These projections are made with a great deal of accuracy, however, since the children who will be going to high school in the '80s are already born. Errors in the figures are possible because the proportion of students that will graduate and the proportion that will go to college may be wrong.

It is hard to know the precise point at which the declining pool will reach a level that will mean difficulties for most schools. The fact is that some schools have already reached a

Table 1

First-time Degree Credit Enrollment Trends to 1986

Birth Year	Births[1] x10³	H.S. Grad Year	H.S. Grads[2] x10³	College Freshman Year	# to College[2] x10³	# to Pub. 4-yr. College[2] x10³	# to Pvt. 4-yr. College[2] x10³	# to Pub. 2-yr. College[2] x10³	# to Pvt. 2-yr. College[2] x10³
1952	3,933	1970	2,896	1970	1,780	737	389	601	53
1953	3,989	1971	2,943	1971	1,766	719	376	620	50
1954	4,102	1972	3,006	1972	1,740	693	372	630	46
1955	4,128	1973	3,039	$973	1,757	706	370	637	45
1956	4,244	1974	3,077	1974	1,854	754	373	682	44
1957	4,332	1975	3,140	1975	1,910	777	386	697	50
1958	4,279	1976	3,135	1976	1,922	781	386	705	50
1959	4,313	1977	3,132	1977	1,933	785	387	711	50
1960	4,301	1978	3,143	1978	1,955	793	388	723	51
1961	4,317	1979	3,127	1979	1,954	793	385	725	51
1962	4,213	1980	3,080	1980	1,936	784	380	722	50
1963	4,142	1981	3,030	1981	1,911	775	373	714	49
1964	4,070	1982	2,941	1982	1,864	754	361	701	48
1965	3,801	1983	2,821	1983	1,787	723	345	673	46
1966	3,642	1984	2m727	1984	1,732	699	331	657	45
1967	3,555	1985	2,679	1985	1,709	640	836	649	44
1968	3,535	1986	2,681	1986					

1. U. S. Bureau of Census, Current Population Reports, Series P-23, No. 49, *Population of the United States, Trends and Prospects: 1950-1990*, (U. S. Government Printing Office, Washington, D. C., 1974)

2. U. S. Department of Health, Education and Welfare, *Projection of Educational Statistics to 1985-86*, 1977 Edition, (U. S. Government Printing Office, Washington, D. C., 1977)

difficult stage, and some have had to close their doors, merely because the rate of increase decreased and the number of high school graduates stabilized. Clearly, some schools have been able to exist in the '70s only because there has been an increasing number of students available for college. The critical stage will, in my opinion, be reached in 1985. At that time there will be a 15% decline in the pool as compared with the number available in 1975. But from now on there will probably be an increasing number of closings of institutions of higher learning, and it is highly likely that the rate of closings will be accelerated after 1985. It is obvious that those institutions whose revenues come primarily from tuition, 80% or more, will be the first schools in trouble.

Many areas, particularly those in the Northeast, will be declining in numbers of high school graduates at a rate higher than the national average. Schools in those areas that have a regional student body and whose revenues come primarily from tuition will get into difficulty most rapidly.

The economy

These demographic changes have implications for the economy that, in turn, have implications for higher education. From 1969 to 1976 the labor force has grown at a rate of 2.3%. As a result of this growth the country has had high rates of unemployment even though the economy has been creating about 2 million new jobs annually. Because of the decline in the number of teenagers, the labor force is expected to grow at only 1.1% in the 1980s. This decline means that, even if the GNP grows at a slower rate, the number of new jobs created will be adequate to absorb the new entrants and keep the unemployment rate at a low level. In other words, the problem of the '80s will likely be a shortage of labor rather than unemployment.[1] The labor shortage may be alleviated by a changed immigration policy and by elimination of the retirement age. Even with such changes it is highly likely that the maintenance of full employment in the economy will not be a major problem. The result of this tendency toward full employment may have some additional negative effects on enrollment. It is likely that high school graduates because of their relative scarcity will command higher salaries, and, unless the percentage increase in salaries of college graduates is even greater, the proportion of high school graduates going to college may be smaller than assumed in Table 1. A similar phenomenon may also reduce the number of college graduates electing graduate school.

The full-employment condition may also have an impact on inflation, which is a major problem for higher education as it is for other sectors of the society. No analysis of inflation satisfies everyone, but I believe there are reasons to be optimistic about its eventual containment. My optimism is based on the fact that government for some time has followed a stop-and-go policy of controlling inflation. Efforts have been made to slow down the rate of inflation through monetary and fiscal policy, but when these efforts have begun to bite and the rate of unemployment has increased, the policies have been reversed in favor of an expansionary policy. If unemployment is not a major problem after 1982, there may be a reduction in expansionary policies and ultimately in inflation. Thus inflation may not be as great an influence on the management of the university in the 1980s as it is currently, at least in the latter half of the 1980s.

Another factor that must be borne in mind is the drive to curb state expenditures. The drive is taking many forms from simple restrictions on the amounts that can be spent to more sophisticated attempts to tie expenditure growth to some measure of economic growth. Regardless of the form of the constraint it is clear that state expenditures for education are not going to keep pace with even a lower rate of inflation through the '80s. Both public and private institutions will be affected by this reduction in the real level of state expenditures.

The management problem in the '80s

Given the condition just described, we have a basis for defining the problems that will be facing the managements of universities in the 1980s. The major problem can be put quite simply, "How can the attention of faculties be kept focused on maintaining excellence in the face of forces pulling the attention to survival?"

The management problem of the '80s will be a struggle to keep the faculty thinking and working on the important problems of education. Faculty members always have difficulty in submerging departmental and professional interests in favor of the interests of the total university. These tendencies will be exacerbated when universities are fighting for their survival or, at best, struggling to preserve a past excellence.

Let us look in more detail at the way a university may be functioning in the '80s, so that we can better appreciate the problem. Because of the demographic changes universities will have a significant financial problem. Traditionally, faculty members ignore the financial condition of the university as a whole on grounds that the problem "is one for administrators to worry about." As the financial problem becomes more severe and impinges directly on faculty welfare, it becomes a faculty problem. This situation is the one most likely to prevail in the '80s.

The financial problem will arise because many schools will fall short of the number of students needed to balance their budgets. As this phenomenon prevails, college and department budgets will be affected. The budgets will be affected because institutions will not be able to compensate for lower numbers by proportionately higher tuitions or proportionally higher levels of state support. In addition, it is unlikely that there will be an increase in giving by individuals and corporations that will compensate for the reduction in numbers of students. The solution will require budget cutting. As this action takes place, the emphasis on survival will become stronger in the minds of faculty members. Those faculty members without tenure will become even more concerned than usual about being able to achieve tenure. Those faculty in departments that have not been attracting students will become concerned about the survival of the department. If there is confidence about survival, then attention will be given to the size of the surviving unit. Similar concerns will be evinced at the level of the college.

The deans of the various colleges will begin to spend their time developing strategies to get a larger share of the smaller quantity of resources in order to maintain the status quo of their units.

As these attitudes develop, the level of internecine conflict will rise at an increasing rate. Competition rather than cooperation will characterize the behavior of faculty and administrators. Departments will contest departments and colleges will challenge colleges. Unfortunately, the negative feelings raised by the conflicts will linger long past the time the conflicts take place. Academic conflicts have a long decay time. The strategy under such circumstances is to look for ways to protect one's position. There is bound to be, under such circumstances, a diminution in the amount of thought dedicated to improving the curriculum and to initiating innovative methods of teaching.

This development has further negative consequences for the particular institution. If education is poorer at a particular school than in the past or than at other schools in competition with it, there will be negative implications for future enrollment. This effect is an example of the vicious cycle phenomenon that organizations may encounter as the environment becomes less benign. Actions that are taken because of adversity result in other actions that make it difficult for the organization to counter the adversity. Such cycles arise in organizations as the organization moves from an equilibrium at a high level of activity to one at a lower level. The problem is to control the movement and to stop it at the appropriate position of adjustment. This description is another way of characterizing certain aspects of the problem of managing universities in the '80s—that is, the problem of attaining a new equilibrium at a smaller scale of operation that is of the same quality as the larger scale.

46

The effects of a poorer economic position will have further deleterious implications for universities. Faculty salaries in the face of inflation and reduced revenue for the university are unlikely to maintain their real value. In addition to the negative impact on faculty morale, the decrease in real faculty salaries further diverts faculty attention from the problem of attaining excellence in the university. The natural reaction to a fall in income is to find a way to rebuild it. For faculty members with outside consulting opportunities, the response will be to increase the amount of time devoted to consulting. Other faculty not usually attracted to consulting will make efforts to find income outside the academy. For the university itself, there will be bad results from the increased consulting of faculty. More attention to nonacademic interests means less attention to education and research—and a reduced commitment to the university. It should be noted that consulting can also be beneficial to a faculty member's professional development. Exposure to problems in the real world can often have a beneficial effect on a professor's teaching and research. Administrators will also be forced to spend more time in outside activities designed to raise more money. The most visible target will probably be government, both federal and state. Both public and private institutions will intensify their efforts to get more government funds. In those states where a subsidy plan for private schools is in existence, usually under the guise of compensation for costs incurred in educating state residents generally or some subset of them, the pressure will be for a higher subsidy. Where one does not already exist, pressure will be put on states to start one. Again this activity takes the time and attention of academic managers away from developing and implementing new ways of achieving greater excellence in education and research.

Economic hardship in academia will also have bad long-run effects, independent of the financial pressure imposed on many institutions, for the academic profession. In an economy where some firms and industries are expanding and represent great potential for the future, a contracting higher education area is not likely to attract the "best and the brightest" from the generation entering the labor market. In an economy where the young are being offered relatively higher salaries because of the demographic changes described above, the decreasing opportunities for tenure, the traditionally lower levels of academic salaries, and the inability of the academy to keep salaries increasing at the rate of inflation are bound to attract proportionally smaller numbers of the most able labor market entrants.

The reduction in the number of people being attracted to the academy occurs at two levels. Fewer PhDs will elect to stay in academic life after they receive their degrees, and fewer students with bachelor degrees will enter graduate school after their first degree. The one exception may be terminal masters degree programs. Since the MBA and other terminal masters degrees have become increasingly good entry points for industry, these programs may well continue to expand in contrast to the general atmosphere of contraction of graduate education expected to prevail. The reduction in the number of graduate students will have some harmful effects on research in science, particularly physics, chemistry, and biology. Faculty members in these disciplines need graduate students to participate in research programs. Without graduate students a faculty member must spend more time in less productive work and in turn will become a less productive researcher. Here again this result has negative financial implications since future research contracts depend on past results. A reduction in research contracts leads to a reduction in the funds available to pay for overhead costs. A smaller pool of graduate students leads to a smaller number of potential academic leaders in the future. Thus for the longer run the education industry will be embarked on a vicious cycle. The financial problems will result in fewer top-quality individuals going into education and, therefore, fewer top-quality people will be available to try to solve the problems. The result is that the problems will tend to grow worse. The net result is a somewhat dismal picture for the future of higher education.

Many distractions exist for faculty in coming years, and it is clear that attention will not be uniquely attracted to excellence. The same condition, however, exists for the managers in the system. We have already described the accelerated need for fund raising at the governmental level. Perhaps the greatest diversion, however, exists in the field of conflict resolution. Academic managers always spend a great deal of time in conflict resolution, but there are two aspects that are expected to be different in the future. First, there will be a significant increase in the number of conflicts arising. The expected reduction (in real terms) of the total pool of resources available will lead to conflicts within and among departments. Second, these conflicts will be more difficult to resolve. In an organization that is receiving an increasing amount of resources, most conflicts can be resolved by a judicious application of more resources. Even when the conflict does not revolve around resources, settlement can be eased by utilizing more resources, frequently as a side payment for one of the parties.[2] Since these conflicts arise because of a diminution of resources, they obviously cannot be settled by this method. The greater difficulty of resolution will result in an increased number of conflicts finding their way to the top of the organization. Deans and department heads will send the problem up the organizational hierarchy. Thus the president of the university will be involved to a greater degree than in the past with conflict resolution at a level of individual problems. That is something that has not been the case historically in most institutions of any size.

The elimination of uncertainty

I have painted a picture that is dismal to say the least. A potential president who believes this portrait of the future is accurate may well go back to being a professor. The other way of looking at the situation is that it represents an ample opportunity for the exercise of one's problem-solving ability and leadership qualities. In any event, it is important that we try to address the situation in a positive manner. Unless we can contribute to the solution of the problems, universities may not be either as plentiful or as effective in the 21st century as in the 20th.

We have said that the greatest problem of university management in the '80s will be maintaining excellence. The danger we must avoid is to allow faculty members, most of whom want to achieve greater excellence for themselves and their university, to suffer frustration in their striving and become willing to compromise their ambitions by settling for mediocrity. The problem at the most general level is to keep the attention-focus of faculty on personal and institutional excellence when all the forces are pulling the faculty member's attention to matters associated with mere survival. The question is, "What can be done by the president and administration?"

The answer lies not in listing actions to take but rather in recognizing the forces acting on the participants in the organization and in attempting to build a different environment. There is clearly no single action that can be taken that will achieve the solution nor is there any unique path to a solution. As a start it is useful to examine the elements that determine attention-focus. Clearly an individual's attention-focus is dependent on his motivation. Maslow has attempted to develop a hierarchy of motives for human beings.[3] Whether or not one is in complete accord with Maslow's theory, there can be no disagreement on the general position that survival is high in any ranking. A person will pay little attention to attaining excellence while his physical survival is still questionable. Similarly, in the circumstances we have described, survival—economic rather than physical—will take precedence over the attainment of excellence. The question of survival arises in the minds of faculty because of the uncertainty generated in the organization, primarily by the enrollment problem. It is the uncertainty that must somehow be attacked. The uncertainty may arise because the faculty does not know how the administration intends to deal with the financial problem created. More specifically, the faculty does not know which of them is likely to be affected by the actions that may be taken. Given the uncertainty of the methods that may be used for solving the problems, the faculty, staff, and students will begin to originate rumors, and these will have the effect of compounding the uncertainty. The university management must deal with the uncertainty directly and as quickly as possible. In fact, the preferable situation is to have a contingency plan developed and ready to be translated into action. The plan should indicate in detail how the administration intends to stabilize the situation when there is a financial problem. The plan should be developed with faculty participation, and the trustees should have the plan explained to them. Quick action and efforts to keep faculty informed are the best deterrents to the expanding uncertainty.

Contingency plans

One difficulty with developing a contingency plan is that those groups that will bear the brunt of budget cuts or a reduction in rates of growth are notified in advance. Indirectly, the president is put in the position of indicating his or her priorities. Some of the sting is reduced by the fact that faculty participate, but, nevertheless, it is hard for those units who are told they must take the most severe financial cuts in case of a problem. However, such a situation is far better than one in which an ad hoc, instant plan attempts to cut every unit proportionally.

Though generating difficulties, an advance plan is clearly better in reducing general uncertainty. The most effective procedure is to develop contingency plans as part of the regular 5-to-10 year financial planning. This can be done most easily by developing alternative plans based on different sets of assumptions. One set should include a pessimistic assumption about enrollment. The resulting budget should be detailed enough to show how funds would be allocated among colleges. Deans in turn should follow through and indicate how they would make allocations among departments. The plans should get down to such details as the desired faculty size under different enrollment assumptions. The point is that concern with survival cannot be eliminated by a pat on the back and reassuring words. It is clear that if enrollment falls, there are going to be some units in the organization that will be hurt. The sooner the information is articulated, the less the shock will be when the action occurs. Bluntness, openness, and frank speaking may be the best antidotes to uncertainty and the resulting difficulties. While not eliminating concern with survival, advance contingency plans may reduce the undesirable faculty behavior that results from contraction. In the final analysis, decisions must be made at a central level and, with advance understanding on the part of the faculty of the kind of decisions that are likely to be made, can reduce the general level of uncertainty.

Management actions for excellence

There are other ways in which the attention-focus of the faculty can be kept on the problem of excellence. Most of these additional methods also involve central actions.

One important type of action involves making additional resources available for educational and research activity. These funds might be made available in the form of an internal organization operated like a foundation. The foundation could entertain proposals for research on education and other subjects. Generally, universities have ignored the need for doing rigorous research on education.[4] By making funds available that might be used for summer salaries or research assistance to faculty who make proposals for the development and implementation of educational ideas, the administration can capture faculty attention and time for work on education. It is useful to have the funds allocated by an internal committee of faculty members as well. The idea of the internal foundation is, of course, to keep the faculty thinking about excellence in education and research. It may seem inconsistent to propose establishing a new activity that uses money to counteract attitudes developing because of a shortage of funds. However, it is important to think in these terms even if the money has to be taken from departmental budgets and, thereby, further aggravates the individual departmental situation. Action must be taken centrally to stimulate the faculty to focus on the basic objectives of the university, and an internal fund for research on education demonstrates the administration's commitment to traditional goals.

In circumstances of the kind we are discussing, it is important for the president and other members of the central administration to use every opportunity, formal and informal, to talk about excellence in education and research. These talks should not be designed as manipulative acts in any sense. But it is only natural when an organization is experiencing financial distress that the president's focus will be on the financial problem also. He should be careful to avoid centering his discussions with the faculty on finances because that will merely accelerate the faculty's concern and will be counterproductive. Thus by writings, speeches, and actions the president and central administration, including the deans and department heads, can help contribute to a concentration on excellence rather than survival. As part of this approach it would be useful to have a concentrated effort, involving faculty, to investigate educational questions and curricula. The aim of such activities is to keep the basic objectives of the organization in front of all the participants. All of these approaches, and many more that could be generated, are designed to counteract the tendency of the faculty to concentrate attention on survival questions rather than questions, of excellence, once financial difficulties beset the institution. Clearly, these approaches will be more effective as the management is able to reduce the general level of uncertainty or to isolate it. As we have seen, however, that is not a simple matter.

Strategic considerations

There are other approaches to the problems of the '80s evolving from the reduction in the available pool of students. One is for the president to recognize that the university will be smaller in the '80s. The tendency of each president is quite the opposite. Each president believes that there will be fewer students available for higher education, but that his or her school will maintain its enrollment. If there is a recognition that enrollment will drop, then it may be possible to calculate the new equilibrium position and move to it gradually rather than abruptly.

The concept of a smaller scale of operations and an equilibrium position of a lower level of operation is hard to comprehend initially because we are conditioned to think in terms of growth. Most universities can be viewed to some extent as modules, and it may be possible to restructure the university, including closing certain buildings, to operate on a smaller scale. It is not possible to reduce all the fixed costs so there will be some minimum size below which an organization cannot operate. It is not obvious where this size is, and it certainly will be different for different institutions.

There are a number of ways to calculate the new equilibrium and, in fact, there are computer models in existence that can be helpful. It is not necessary to reinvent the wheel completely. Since the driving force in the contemplated change is the enrollment, the best approach is to start with an estimate of the enrollment that can be maintained as the available pool of students decreases. Fortunately, the available numbers of high school graduates that will be present in the '80s have been experienced in the past. From Table 1, column 4, the reader can verify that 1980 and 1974 are similar as are 1981 and 1973 and 1982 and 1971. Further pairings can be made by going back to the sixties. By utilizing share of market data or some other technique, it should be possible to get an estimated enrollment for each year of the '80s. I do not mean to say that each year will be similar to a year in the past, but the past data does give a starting point. Clearly, there are variables in the picture that are difficult to predict, such as the proportion of men and women deciding

56

to go on to college. Once the enrollment has been determined, the size of faculty necessary to teach that size student body can be calculated by using historical faculty-student ratios. Obviously, this formulation is a simplified version of the problem, but it should be clear that a new equilibrium can be calculated. The point is that the university can be rescaled to a smaller size with all of the interrelationships among the units taken into account.

There is clearly a strong element of the status quo assumed, but that can be dealt with as the basis for change develops. The university then has a target to shrink toward and can start immediately. The first steps, and the most difficult ones, have to be taken with faculty. Knowing the size faculty needed by 1985, it is possible to estimate the number of tenured faculty that will be appropriate, and actions can be taken to move toward that number. Obviously, it is not pleasant to be restrictive before one has to do so, but it is usually better to have evolutionary rather than radical change.

There is one correction that should be noted. The concept of a new equilibrium implies some stability, but a glance at Table I indicates that the number of high school graduates continues to diminish each year. Thus universities may experience a moving equilibrium. This continued reduction in the pool of students may mean that any equilibrium is valid for only a few years, and then a new position must be specified. That situation is possible, but it is also likely that the enrollment may stabilize for the surviving private schools. As capacity is reduced in the private sector, there will be more students available for the remaining schools. Therefore, the situation may not be as bleak as it might seem.

There are other approaches that can be taken once a future decline in students is recognized. The most popular remedy suggested by many people is to shift age groups. If the 17-to-21 age group is decreasing in size, the advice to schools is to shift to the older groups where there are more people. Some schools have taken this advice already. For those schools who can do so, nothing is wrong in servicing an older group. Many schools, however, cannot make this shift easily. In particular, universities having an emphasis on professional education may have difficulties in making a transition to older students. Where the older student is prepared to adapt to the existing curriculum, there is no problem. If the university has to develop special courses with less technical content, there will clearly be difficulties. My view is that the older student will not be a solution for most universities.

In research universities, one strategic change a president may make is to reduce the teaching faculty and to increase the research faculty. There is some evidence already developing that there may be more research funds available in certain areas at the same time that the supply of students is decreasing. Thus it may be possible to shift some tenured faculty away from teaching to full-time research and also to increase the number of nontenured faculty doing full-time research. Such shifts are predicated on the assumption that outside research funds can be found to finance the research. These shifts make sense for research universities that believe their enrollments will decrease. Basically, they are becoming somewhat more like research institutes and a little less like universities. The shift violates the principle that most research universities establish—namely, that all faculty should both teach and do research. On the whole, this kind of strategic shift makes sense if the outside funding exists. It is always possible to make the shift back as students become more plentiful. It is a healthy form of adaptation because it enables the university to remain viable and contribute to society without violating its basic objectives.

Other management problems of the '80s

Part of the strategy of maintaining an emphasis on excellence requires attention to the problem of faculty development. Programs for sabbaticals need to be maintained. The automatic sabbatical for each faculty member after seven years of service is a luxury that may not be maintainable for many schools in a period of financial stringency. This loss may not be as great as it may seem as long as a program of sabbaticals based on the merit of the individual and the proposal is substituted. Emphasis on merit again brings faculty attention to the objective of excellence in personal and institutional achievement. Where funds cannot be allocated in sufficient amounts to finance the merit sabbatical, it is possible through utilizing different teaching loads and the trading of teaching to enable the program to exist. The better the faculty, of course, the more likely the individual is to receive outside financing for the leave.

Perhaps the second most serious problem of the '80s is maintaining the integrity of the university while surviving. Since enrollments are going to be the most important variable affecting the university, there will always be temptations to adopt actions that are designed to save the university, but many of these actions will only demean it. As an example, let us look at the following quote from a college that was suffering and called in consultants for advice. One consultant suggested that the institution "should proceed as though it were starting an entirely new college: study the potential market to determine what students and their parents want, redesign the college to meet those wants, and recruit for a freshman class in 1981."

This college was on the verge of closing and was far below the size necessary to maintain its viability. The consultant was trying desperately to find measures that might resuscitate it. But it is important to recognize the difference between prostitution and adaptation. There are some actions no organization (or individual) should take merely to survive. In education, it is crucial that educators remain in command of the curriculum and programs of study. To turn a liberal arts college into a vocational school because a survey shows that is the desire of potential students is wrong. One year later the fad may be in another direction and, following the same principle, the school should again become something new. As educators we must be responsible for maintaining standards and a professional approach. Catering to whims shows a lack of integrity. Conserving the past for tradition's sake shows a lack of adaptability. Good educational programs cannot be designed on the basis of survey data. Useful knowledge about the way in which potential students view an institution may be gained from surveys and used to improve the written material describing the institution. Educators must be sensitive to the needs of students, but the educators must make the decisions affecting education on educational criteria, not survey data.

There are other threats to the integrity of the university. The heavy emphasis on jobs among students has led institutions to advertise to employers and students in the ways that make the educational institution appear to be nothing more than a commercial factory.

Pressure on faculty members to get research grants leads in some cases to the acceptance of research that should not be done in a university. The pressure from money has in the past and will in the future lead universities in directions that threaten the concept of a university as an educational institution.

In order to keep the university from being driven to taking questionable actions, the president must have a clear set of objectives for the university. These objectives must be developed in conjunction with the deans and department heads and must be understood by the faculty. These objectives can serve as criteria to guide decisions on new activities. The objectives can serve as a picture of the kind of organization the university wants to be. The members of the university community must understand the nature of the university as it is currently and the kind of institution it is trying to become.

Governmental relations will clearly be an ever-enlarging problem. Private schools will undoubtedly have an increasing interaction with state governments and, of course, the public institutions, by their nature, must have. The institutions in both sectors will have to work together to develop some orderly ways to shrink capacity. We have seen that there must be a reduction in capacity, but at this time it is likely that the shrinkage will take place primarily in the private sector. Some criteria need to be developed so that the educational system as a whole will be of higher quality after the shrinkage than before. Relations with the federal government will inevitably increase also. The increases will come because of increased aid to education and because of increased regulation. The increase in aid will develop because of the plight of an increasing number of schools and the inability or unwillingness of state governments to involve themselves more deeply in higher education. There is no question that the "Proposition 13" syndrome will persist in many different forms at the state level. The increase in regulation from the federal government is likely because of the increased aid and because of the many regulations on the books that have not yet been applied to higher education. Given time and enough bureaucrats, government will undoubtedly apply the regulations. The attention we are paying to the problem of government regulation now will probably have a good effect and reduce the rate of increase, but regulation will not go away.

The problem of continuing to attract bright, young people to the academy is a serious problem for the '80s. We have discussed a number of reasons why the supply will decrease but have not presented any solutions. It is obvious that the only way academia can attract the young is through increasing the job opportunities available for them. Through an organization like NSF it is possible to have some effect on demand. A number of schemes such as new research institutes can help increase opportunities, but some things can be done by individual institutions as well. Perhaps the most significant action can be taken in the area of part-time faculty. With a financial squeeze there is a natural tendency to move to part-time people in many fields. They are cheaper teachers on a per-course basis. However, we need to look hard at this practice and attempt to consolidate some of the funds allocated to part-time people. These funds might then be used to hire more young people. We must find ways to increase the demand, or universities will suffer in the long run.

Leadership versus Management

Up to this point we have stressed the concept of management in this essay. It is clear that management is of crucial importance if universities are to make a smoother transition to the 1980s.

However, there are significant differences between management and leadership, and both qualities will be necessary if presidents are to be effective in the 1980s. Management is the art of allocating resources within the organization in a manner designed to reach the goals of the organization. Management techniques concentrate on developing the most effective and efficient usage of resources within the organization, including human resources.

It is possible to be an effective manager without being an effective leader. A manager may balance the budget but make little or no progress in improving the organization so that it is capable of achieving greater objectives.

Leadership is the art of stimulating the human resources within the organization to concentrate on total organizational goals rather than on individual or subgroup goals. Participants in every organization tend to form subgroups with individuals having similar goals to their own.

These goals are often in conflict with the goals of the total organization. The art of leadership is to convince the participants to modify their goals so that they conform with those of the total organization and to put their efforts into helping the total organization achieve its goals.

Occasionally, a manager can do some of this by virtue of the authority given to him by his organizational role. In general, however, leadership requires more than the authority given by the organizational role. The leader must articulate a set of goals for the total organization that capture the imagination of the participants and induce them to forsake their personal and subgroup goals to enlist in the cause of the total organization. Leadership requires the manager to take initiative, to be articulate, and to be convincing. Leadership is being proactive rather than reactive. Leaders mobilize the human resources of the organization, managers the nonhuman.

Conclusion

We have described some of the characteristics of the '80s and have atttempted to demonstrate how these characteristics will affect universities. In general, we have painted a gloomy picture. Universities will be faced with lower enrollments, which will lead to financial problems. We did not dwell on the fact that there is little hope that private giving will increase enough to compensate. There can be some hope that if inflation abates, as predicted, that securities markets might improve and enable endowment incomes to increase. But when all variables are taken into account, it is still true that universities will be struggling financially. The danger is that the condition will divert faculty members from concentrating on excellence in education and research. For a variety of reasons it is reasonable to expect strong tendencies in that direction. We then went through a number of actions that might be taken now and when the crisis occurs to alleviate or eliminate some of the problems.

All of the proposed solutions, however, were characterized by one common element. They all require strong leadership from the president. Management in the '80s must be more centralized than has traditionally been the case. In the '80s, presidents must again become educational leaders in their institutions. Even fund-raising activities may have to take a back seat to the necessity of having the president function as an intellectual leader. In their actions and in their utterances, the presidents must embody the search of excellence that they want and need in faculty members. No longer can the president be strictly an outside person. The demands of the inside are going to overwhelm the demands of the outside. The president will need to write more and speak more to the faculty in large and small groups. Only through such intense activity can the university remain a viable institution in the society. If the battle for excellence is forsaken for survival, universities will not survive. Without the president at the head of the line, the faculty will not follow. The demands on the president will be greater than the heavy ones imposed in the '60s and '70s. It will clearly be a time for presidents who can lead and act, and the prize is the continued life and progress of the university itself.

Notes

(¹) See A. R. Weber, "The Changing Labor Market Environment," Carnegie-Mellon University, 1978. To be published by Bobbs-Merrill Company, Inc. as part of the Key Issues series at New York University.

(²) *Cf.* R. M. Cyert and J. G. March, *A Behavioral Theory of the Firm* (Englewood Cliffs, N.J.: Prentice-Hall, Inc., 1963).

(³) Abraham Maslow, *Motivation and Personality* (New York: Harper & Row, 1954).

(⁴) See Bat-Sheva Eylon and F. Reif, "Effects of Internal Knowledge Organization Task Performance," paper presented at the annual meeting of the American Educational Research Association, April 1979.

Richard M. Cyert, Ph.D., is the President of Carnegie-Mellon University. The recipient of both of Ford and Guggenheim Foundation Fellowship, Dr. Cyert is the author of **Management of Non-Profit Organizations: With Emphasis on Universities** *and of numerous articles on business management and organizational theory.*

Leadership: An Attempt to Look At the Future

by Gene I. Maeroff

The outlines of the scenario are gradually taking shape. . .

- A declining number of high school graduates.
- A shortage of labor.
- A drive to curb public expenditures.

Richard M. Cyert filled in the details in a paper unveiled one rainy morning last spring in downtown Boston. What he described was something less foreboding than the threat posed by the Four Horsemen of the Apocalypse, but it was nonetheless unnerving to anyone concerned with the future of higher education. Mr. Cyert's vision of the 1980s includes glimpses of faculties wondering how to preserve excellence when survival itself is in question, institutions struggling to enroll enough students to balance their budgets, departments fighting departments and colleges battling colleges, professors turning increasingly to outside pursuits to supplement salaries that are losing ground in real buying power, and, ultimately, fewer top-quality people making their careers in what appears to them to be an enterprise in decline.

Enter the Institute for Educational Management. What role will there be during the next decade for a program designed to help senior-level college and university administrators develop and enhance their skills in effective leadership and management? This is the question that 14 men and 1 woman gathered around a table at the Harvard Club to try to answer. They were brought together by IEM to conduct a Symposium on Leadership that could provide the Institute with guidance in shaping its future. What the participants had in common were their professional background in higher education and a history of having thought about the state of the field.

The basis for the day's discussion was a pair of papers that Chris Argyris and Mr. Cyert had been invited to prepare. The deliberations that began over juice and muffins that morning will turn out to be wasted, of course, in the event that two or three thousand Winston Churchill-types should be available to run the nation's institutions of higher education during the 1980s. That unlikely eventuality aside, some rather unusual qualities will have to be cultivated in the people who occupy the posts.

More than anything else, the conversation revolved around the issue of management vs. leadership. Should the two qualities be given equal weight? Which will be more important? Can they be combined in a single individual? "In the 1960s and the 1970s," Dean Currie said, "lots of management was needed. Values and assumptions remained constant, but institutions had to grow. The 1980s will require challenges to values and assumptions, and that will require leadership."

The debate was pursued in a spirit of collegiality. There were no barbs or sharp exchanges. Despite the many prophecies about higher education in the next decade, uncertainty still prevails, and it was as though everyone was acknowledging that this was a joint venture into the unknown. Yet the passion of exploration was missing. The coffee was consumed and the quips were exchanged, but seldom did strong feelings show themselves. Ultimately, the sense of the symposium, reached by default rather than by declaration, was that it would be a mistake for IEM to lean too heavily in either direction, that the challenge of the 1980s will require both management and leadership.

It took hours of probing and testing before the participants converged on this idea. "I feel uncomfortable with the distinction that's being made between leadership and management," Willard Enteman said at one point, abruptly yanking the participants out of the dichotomy into which they had been descending. It was a definitive statement of the sort heard all too infrequently through the day. Often, the conversation remained unfocused and there was little effort by the participants to hold each other accountable.

Nolen Ellison, the only participant providing the symposium with the community college perspective, reminded the others that many of the two-year institutions are only now reaching the level of maturity that the four-year institutions attained years ago. Thus, while some educators may feel that the era of management has passed, those in the two-year sector may not agree.

Joe Nyquist, never one to avoid a controversy, seized

on what he called "a glaring contradiction" in Mr. Cyert's presentation. "You talk about needing tough managers and yet in the closing comments you talk about the need for intellectual leaders." Such challenges were scarce, however, and if the participants felt a sense of excitement over the topic, they never really showed it. The grayness of the day, as perceived from the 38th floor of an office tower that poked into the rain-filled clouds, seemed to pervade the meeting.

It was clear, though, that the participants felt that the emergence of leadership in the colleges and universities of the 1980s will be tied to the ability to make tough decisions. There will be a need for men and women who can swing support to unpopular causes. Much to their credit, the symposium participants shunned the overworked word *retrenchment*, but the message was there all the same.

Not just any administrator will be able to raise delicate questions about the tenure system. Not just any administrator will be able to get departments to reduce their course offerings. Not just any administrator will be able to turn down proposals to dilute academic programs when those proposals are sure-fire methods of producing desperately needed tuition dollars. Leadership, in other words, will be the sine qua non of change.

"The question of how you bring about change in an organization is particularly relevant for the 1980s because we are going to have to have changes, and some of those changes may be radical," observed Mr. Cyert. He might have added that some of those changes will be ones that nobody wants but that everybody realizes are essential.

Even in light of the readily demonstrated need for change, Frank Newman and others foresaw difficulties.

"There is a process in American life," Mr. Newman observed, "that contains a powerful sense of antileadership. Just wait for any president to mention tenure, for instance, and they are off to draw blood. A lot of a president's time is spent managing the antileadership problem. This phenomenon is not peculiar to higher education."

Stephen K. Bailey, whose patient style provided the fulcrum on which he balanced the various points of view as moderator of the symposium, amplified Mr. Newman's remarks. "Today," he said, "there often is no sense that anyone is in charge. There was once some degree of hierarchic power and whether you liked the person at the top of the hierarchy or not, you didn't take him on."

The leadership vacuum was what some participants had in mind. Perhaps higher education could use a few people like Fred Shero, individuals who can place themselves firmly in control and turn around a situation in short order. Mr. Shero is a hockey genius who made a loser into a winner in a single season as coach of the New York Rangers. He has the ability to spot weaknesses, implement changes, motivate his followers, and keep morale from disintegrating. The task facing top administrators at colleges and universities during the coming decade will be similar.

Surely, as competition among institutions of higher education grows more fierce, there will be a need for leaders who are willing to pinpoint and denounce practices that are not in the public interest. If the higher education profession itself does not produce these crusaders, then they will come from some other sector of society. This is an issue that was introduced at the symposium and surely one that should be on the agenda of IEM, but the participants presented no new ideas about how IEM could address such concerns.

"The university is one of the most resistant organizations to change," Paul Ylvisaker said. "When people are hired into academic life, they are hired on the basis of what they can contribute as individuals. They are chosen for performance and for loyalty to a guild, and their loyalties are not confined to the institution. This is the constituency with which an administration must deal in trying to get the organization to change."

What emerged in the minds of the participants as a main obstacle to leadership is an atmosphere in which many issues simply are not discussed. Apparently, the marketplace of free ideas is not all that open. While this may also be true in many other fields, there is the possibility that higher education may have more than its share of hidden agendas. How is a leader to lead if he cannot face the issues head-on, if he is not permitted to raise certain questions?

Kenneth Ashworth told of the situation at the publicly supported institutions of Texas, where, he said, "there is a definite need for the presidents to find the right agenda. But there are a lot of nondiscussable issues. Information is useful and they don't want to share it." Mr. Ashworth even had trouble arranging a conference at which the presidents were to talk openly with governing board members about the implications of declining enrollments. The governing board members had never been given the full story. The presidents did not want to open this can of worms in front of the governing board members. Perhaps the presidents thought that enrollments would stop declining if only they didn't talk about what was happening.

In such a setting, not just any process will break down the wall of conspiracy and lead to meaningful and substantial change. Mr. Argyris's paper spoke of "double-loop learning," a rather arcane concept, as the means of lifting the curtain on the nondiscussable. The theory was examined gingerly by the participants, few of them apparently willing to admit that the idea was difficult to grasp. Mr. Cyert, however, confessed, "I had trouble understanding what you meant, Chris." Mr. Enteman, Mr. Currie, and one or two others entered the fray, but most felt more comfortable listening to Mr. Argyris trying to explain the obtuseness of the paper.

"People have theories in their heads that are counter-productive to what I call double-loop learning," he said. "You have to keep looking at underlying assumptions. The games that people have played for the last 20 years are not going to be possible in the administration of higher education in the future."

Double-loop learning, it seems, is a process that is supposed to get the hidden agenda onto the table where it can be seen and discussed. It is a matter of getting people to acknowledge their motives. Otherwise, according to Mr. Argyris, decisions are made for reasons other than those stated, and the result is single-loop learning. Mr. Argyris cited the example of the mathematics department at a famous university, where the appointment of a professor was opposed by the faculty on the ground that "he would not fit in." As it turned out, the issue actually revolved around a nondiscussable dispute over whether the department should swing toward pure or applied mathematics. But the underlying controversy was not acknowledged.

Going on to another example that he thought would elaborate on his point, Mr. Argyris spoke of the recent critical report that Derek Bok, Harvard's president, wrote of the Business School. "There are many faculty members at the Business School who could have written that report, but they would have died rather than do it," Mr. Argyris asserted. Again, the nondiscussable stood in the way of double-loop learning.

Another Harvard report, the proposal for revamping the core curriculum, was discussed by the participants as a possible example of double-loop learning. But they could not agree on whether it was double-loop or single-loop because they were uncertain about the amount of openness that characterized the development of the report. Mr. Enteman suspected that there was something Machiavellian about Dean Henry Rosovsky's role, rendering the process single-loop, rather than double-loop. In other words, the action was taken, but all of the chips may not have been on the table.

The matter of candor was a recurring theme of the day's deliberations. The relationship between candor and leadership seemed to intrigue the participants, and given more time, they might have delved more deeply into the issue. As it was, Mr. Nyquist predicted that moral leadership will be in short supply during the 1980s. "We will need people," he said, "with the ability to manage decline gracefully and with some dignity and with constructive candor." The discussion might easily have moved toward an examination of the impact of candor on leadership in an era in which it will be incumbent on some presidents to admit that their institutions and their constituents would be better served by closing down the most troubled schools. Such a discussion never developed, however.

Richard Bjork broached the pragmatic, asking whether IEM would be doing top administrators a favor by teaching them to be candid and then sending them back to their campuses to practice what they have learned, only to see them "get shot down."

"Nothing in my paper says go ahead and be a damned fool," said Mr. Argyris, whose double-loop concept is ostensibly built on honesty. Obviously, the topic could have used more airing.

The discussion of double-loop learning so dominated the morning session of the symposium that Mr. Bailey found it necessary to put a time limit on the topic. What sometimes seemed to be missing was a recognition by the participants that they were brought together to help set a foundation for IEM's future. Interesting as the conversation may have been, there was a disappointing failure to link up the issues with IEM's program. A lunch of cantelope and salad, served in the meeting room to allow the deliberations to continue, appeared to give the participants the break they needed to begin zeroing in on the needs of IEM. Considerable sympathy developed for the notion of at least leaving IEM with a sort of framework that the Institute could give to administrators as a guide to the decision-making process.

This need was underlined by Frederic Jacobs, who pointed out that half of IEM's participants have been from colleges with enrollments of fewer than 2,000. "Many of them work in severe isolation," he said. "They are very much by themselves and go back to their campuses and have no one with whom to share their new assumptions."

How to keep in touch with IEM's graduates and how to carry the message of IEM to a wider audience were the crucial questions for which only the beginnings of answers were provided. Consideration was given to the possibility of a journal modeled after the *Harvard Business Review*, a series of cassettes that educators could listen to at their own

75

convenience, more short seminars in Cambridge, and road shows across the country.

But this observer felt as the hour of adjournment was approaching that the assembled expertise had not been used to its full potential. Much of what was propounded could have been formulated just as easily—and at less expense to IEM—by the Institute's own staff over a few bottles of Heineken in a Harvard Square tavern. Perhaps the symposium might have been structured differently to engender more insightful thinking. Or maybe people with a different perspective are needed to think creatively about the 1980s. Or it could have been that a sunny day would have been more productive than an overcast one.

The conclusions were scanty. IEM's role for the 1980s is still under consideration and Richard Chait emphasized that he would welcome a candid consideration of the possibilities. "Do you see any evidence that IEM does any good at all?" he asked earnestly of the symposium. "Maybe people should come to IEM for credentials or maybe they should come for six weeks of vacation or maybe for the opportunity to find a new position. Maybe there is very little we can teach them. Maybe we are running it for the wrong people. Maybe we should be running it for key faculty, members of the legislature, the media, and key students."

Thus, IEM is entering its second decade with the kind of openness that would make the Institute a welcome candidate for double-loop learning. One wonders in reflection how Mr. Argyris would have rated the symposium as a double-loop exercise. By the time that the symposium adjourned, the skies above Boston had cleared and the golden dome of the State House, obscured by mist most of the day, was now visible in all its glory. It could not be immediately determined whether the symbolism was lost on the participants, who had repaired to other environs of the Harvard Club for liquid refreshment.

Gene Maeroff is the National educational correspondent for the New York Times. *He writes on nationwide developments in elementary and secondary schools, as well as on those in colleges and universities.*

I𝐄M

Symposium on Leadership

PARTICIPANTS

Chris Argyris
Conant Professor of Education and
Organizational Behavior
Harvard Graduate School of Education

Kenneth Ashworth
Commissioner, Coordinating Board
Texas College and University System

Stephen K. Bailey
Professor of Education and Social Policy
Harvard Graduate School of Education
(Formerly, Vice President
American Council on Education)

Richard Bjork
Chancellor
Vermont State Colleges

Richard Chait
Educational Chairman
Institute for Educational Management
Harvard Graduate School of Education

Dean Currie
Assistant Dean for Educational Affairs
Harvard Graduate School of
Business Administration

Richard Cyert
President
Carnegie-Mellon University

Nolen Ellison
Chancellor
Cuyahoga Community College District
Central Office (Cleveland, Ohio)

Willard Enteman
President
Bowdoin College

Frederic Jacobs
Administrative Director
Institute for Educational Management
Assistant Dean for Programs
in Professional Education
Harvard Graduate School of Education

Gene I. Maeroff
National Education Correspondent
The New York Times

Frank Newman
President
University of Rhode Island

Ewald Nyquist
Vice President
Pace University
(Formerly, Commissioner of Education,
State of New York)

Blenda Wilson
Senior Associate Dean
Harvard Graduate School of Education

Paul Ylvisaker
Dean
Havard Graduate School of Education

Institute for
Educational Management

The Institute for Educational Management offers an opportunity for senior level college and university administrators to develop and enhance their skills in effective leadership and management. Founded in 1970, IEM is offered jointly by the Harvard Graduate Schools of Business Administration and Education.

The Institute presents a 6-week comprehensive program of intensive training. IEM offers its program as a broadening experience dealing with problems such as financial management, labor relations, government regulations, use of management information systems, and increased litigation. Since 1970, more than 1000 college and university administrators from nearly 500 institutions have attended IEM. Participants are drawn nationally from all sectors of postsecondary education.

IEM is designed for senior level administrators at postsecondary institutions; the Institute seeks to serve primarily those individuals whose current responsibilities and authority affect institutional policy.

337 Gutman Library
Appian Way
Cambridge, MA 02138